A-IN THE LAP OF ATHENA

Author
Gill Goddard

Illustrations
Maggie Downer

Published by
Scholastic Publications Ltd,
Villiers House,
Clarendon Avenue,
Leamington Spa,
Warwickshire CV32 5PR

© 1995 Scholastic Publications Ltd

The author wishes to thank Pat Hughes for her valuable help.

Designed using Aldus Pagemaker
Printed in Great Britain by Ebenezer Baylis, Worcester
British Library Cataloguing-in-Publication Data
A catalogue record for this book is available from the British Library.

ISBN 0-590-53335-5

Picture references

Ancient Art & Architecture p11, p13, p19, p23, p24, p25, p27, p31; Bridgeman Art Library p5, p14; British Museum p3, p28; C M Dixon p22; Mary Evans Picture Library p2, p29; Giraudon/Bridgeman Art Library p9, p19; Greg Evans, p10, p16; Michael Holford p15; Mansell Collection p7; Spectrum Colour Library, p20; Werner Forman Archive/British Museum, London p8.

This story is set in 480BC. At this time Ancient Greece was divided up into city states which were run independently by *archons*, officials chosen by the citizens. Athens was one of the largest.

Citizens could vote in all the assemblies where decisions were made about the way things were run in the city. This gave them the power to change things. However, not everyone was a citizen. Non-citizens included aliens, the name given to people from other places who lived and worked in the city, usually traders. Also, women were not citizens. They had no vote and they could not own property.

Finally there were slaves. These were owned by their masters and had no rights, although they could be freed by their masters. Sometimes, they were treated very badly, sometimes they became trusted friends. Like Sicinnus in the story, they were often prisoners of war. They were trusted to do very responsible jobs like teach or supervise children. Some could read and write and acted as scribes.

At the time of this story Greece was being threatened by Persia, a large country to the east of Greece. The Persians had a big army and navy and they were a great danger to the small city states.

Ten years earlier the Athenians had won an outstanding victory in extraordinary circumstances at Marathon to the north-east of the city. It stopped the Persian attack but now their leader, King Xerxes, was leading a second attack on Greece.

His forces swept through the city states, conquering each in turn. The Persian forces were halted temporarily by a tiny force of Spartan soldiers led by Leonidas who met the Persian army in a narrow pass between mountains at Thermopylae. They held them back for several days but all the Spartan soldiers died. Eventually, the Persian army found a way across the mountains and headed south.

Athens was a major target. Themistocles, who had earlier persuaded the Greeks to build a navy, helped to organize the defence of the city by persuading the citizens to agree to the evacuation of women and children to a town in the south. Then, when the Persians were about to attack the city, he used the Greek fleet to transport everyone left to the island of Salamis.

The Battle of Salamis is a documented historical event and we also know that Themistocles was the mastermind behind it.

The fact that Themistocles appears on an Ancient Greek coin confirms his reputation as an important Athenian Commander.

Finally it was his plan to trick the much larger fleet of Persian ships into entering the narrow seas between the Greek mainland and Salamis. He used his Persian slave, Sicinnus to pass false information on to the Persian forces and so bring them to the straits of Salamis. It worked. The battle was chaotic but in the end the Greeks won and the Persians pulled back.

Athens was badly burnt but was rebuilt.

We know about Themistocles from Plutarch, a Roman historian, writing 500 years later. He used the information he found in writings to tell us about Themistocles and his part in the defence of Athens. He tells us also that Themistocles had ten children in all. All we know of the children are their names and that the first son died in an accident with a horse. The second son was adopted by his grandfather, a normal situation at that time. At the time of the story these children were thought to be part of Themistocles' family:

Boys	Girls
Archeptolis(Archie)	Italia
Polyeuctus (Pol)	Sybaris (Syb)
Cleophantus (Cleo)	

We know that Sicinnus was a trusted slave, a prisoner of war captured by Themistocles at the battle of Marathon and tutor to the children.

Life was very different then to our lives today. All children were brought up to know the stories of their gods and to attend many religious festivals each year. The boys would learn by heart many of the stories from Homer's *Iliad* and *Odyssey*, stories about famous heroes who the children were supposed to copy in their courage and morals.

Women and girls however were not considered equal to men. They could not vote, could not own property and belonged to their male relatives or husband. They were kept in the house and yard and hardly ever went out, then only with a male escort. Women were seldom educated and married very young, often between fourteen and sixteen years of age to a man in his thirties. Women ran the house, cooked and made the clothes.

Myths and legends used in the story

Homer's Iliad

This tells the tale of the Greek siege of Troy and the incident of the wooden horse. It starts when King Agamemnon kidnaps Chryseis the daughter of a high priest. Achilles, a young hero, tries to persuade the king to let her go but he won't. The priest calls on the gods to cause trouble for the king in his attack on Troy. The story poem tells about these troubles.

In the diary Cleo talks of the time when Achilles, a young lad at the time, tries to get out of fighting on King Agamemnon's side. His parents send him disguised as a girl into the women's quarters of King Lykomedes. Unfortunately he is found out and required to go and fight for King Agamemnon.

Homer's Odyssey

This is the story of a hero, Odysseus, who sets sail from Troy to go home. His journey is beset by storms, shipwreck, giants and sea creatures and it takes him ten years to get home. His wife Penelope waits at home for him and weaves her tapestry. Pressure is out on her to marry someone else but she says she will not choose a new husband until the tapestry is complete. She weaves during the day and undoes all her work at night so that she doesn't have to marry. Odysseus' faithful hound who guards the gate to Penelope's palace is called Argos.

Jason and the Argonauts

Jason is dared by his evil uncle, who has taken his father's rightful place as king, to find the Golden Fleece. If he does so, his father will be restored as king. The Golden Fleece is a sacred coat of a ram that could fly. Jason sets off in his ship, the Argo, and he and his men, the Argonauts, are beset by many adventures. His final challenge comes when he is attacked by the dragon that guards the fleece.

Diary of Cleo, son of Themistocles, 481-480 BC

October 14
(the year before the 75th Olympiad)

I must have looked like the boy in this statue as I raced towards the finishing line.

Today, at last, Sicinnus, our slave tutor, let me try horse-racing. We were at the palaestra this afternoon when the horses were brought in to allow the riders a chance to practise their races for the Games.

One of the boys fell awkwardly and twisted his arm. I begged the Games Master to let me take his place. For a long moment I thought he wouldn't agree, but then Sicinnus nodded so he hoisted me up on to the back of the black stallion.

It took a while to bring the horse under my command I admit, but I was able to take my place at the starting line for the next race. It was a sprint, the length of the stadium, no turns, easy. Well, sort of.

The horse snorted and pranced and tried to toss me off but then we started to gallop. We flew like the wind, me crouching low and hanging on for dear life. The thunderous noise of hooves was deafening. Sand was thrown up in our faces, blinding us. It was madness but brilliant. We surged ahead, flank to flank with our main rival. I urged the horse on, harder and harder, driving my heels into his sides and desperately trying to stay on at the same time. We crossed the line first! The horse swerved violently and I didn't. I shot forward and crashed to the ground landing in a sprawling heap by the wall!

But I won, I won and at the first attempt! At last I've found something I can do better than my brothers. They've beaten me at everything! But not this. None of them have risked the horse-racing.

Sicinnus picked me up, checked me for breaks and grinned when he was sure I was in one piece. I laughed, what else could I do?

It hurt, even after I'd been in the baths and Sicinnus had oiled and massaged me but it was well worth it.

October 15

This is stupid! Mother caught sight of my bruises this morning while I was washing in the courtyard with my brothers. She yanked me upright and demanded to know what I'd done to be so badly marked.

I didn't think she would object to the horse-racing but when I told her she went wild. She sent for Sicinnus and yelled at him, threatening to have him beaten for allowing me to race.

He kept silent and did not flinch even when she hit him. He could have killed her with his bare hands. He was a fine soldier of the Persian army, captured and enslaved by my father at the Battle of Marathon.

I screamed at her to stop but she turned on me and struck me, knocking me to the ground. Archie, my oldest brother, picked me up but I could tell he was shaken.

Father's voice rang out across the courtyard. He strode towards us and reached for mother's wrist, heaving her away from me and towards the living room. They disappeared inside and we all breathed a sigh of relief.

Sicinnus was so calm. He coolly told my brothers to get their bags for school and wait by the doorway. He threw my tunic and cloak to me and told me to get dressed quickly.

I felt wretched all of a sudden. I wanted to be sick. Sicinnus must have seen it because he gave me a swig of wine from an amphora and ruffled my hair.

When we got home for dinner at noon, mother wasn't there. Father sent the girls away to their nurse after dinner and quietly explained to us that my oldest brother, Neocles, had died being trampled in a horse-race. He was mother's first-born son. That's why she was so upset.

'But I can race, can't I? Please father!' I pleaded. This was my only chance to be great, to win the olive wreath.

Father didn't answer at once. He was serious and lost that smile he usually had in his eyes. I saw him glance momentarily at Sicinnus, then he agreed but issued a warning.

'No boasting at home, Cleo. Don't talk about it at all in your mother's hearing, or it ends.'

I nodded furiously. Father got up to go but I had to ask one more question.

The painting on this vase provides clues about school life in Ancient Greece.

'Sicinnus won't be beaten, will he?'

'No' father replied with a smile that made me feel much better.

I wasn't allowed to go to the gym this afternoon. Sicinnus said I wasn't fit and he wouldn't be persuaded. So I played with my sisters Syb and Italia.

Syb's just five and she makes me laugh. We played chase and then I pushed her on the swing until I got tired.

She's got a dog called Argos. He's great fun. I taught him to jump through a hoop. It made Syb giggle.

Italia looked on with that silly 'I'm too grown up for such games' expression on her face. She's twelve, a year older than me. I splashed her with water from the courtyard fountain and that stopped her nonsense. She gave chase and she's fast! We ended up collapsed in a heap laughing too much to wrestle and with Argos barking and jumping all over us.

My sisters enjoy playing knucklebones like the girls in this statue. I prefer to run and wrestle!

Helen, our nurse, rescued me from Italia's grasp. Clipping me gently around the ear, she sent me off to the kitchen for some food and as I went, I heard poor Italia getting a long lecture about behaving properly! I'm glad I'm not a girl. They never have any fun, stuck indoors with their weaving and baking.

December 10

Sicinnus has promised to teach me archery. He's a brilliant archer. Father agreed and I've to have my first lesson tomorrow. We're going outside the city walls into the countryside. I shall be riding one of father's horses and he's going to come with us. My brother Pol is coming too but Archie is a serious contender for the boy's sprint at the Olympic Games so he's spending most of his time at the gym and stadium practising.

December 11

I hit something! I actually managed to hit something with my arrow. It wasn't what I was aiming at but I killed a hare with one shot nonetheless. We had the hare for supper!

I like archery! I shall lead the first archery column in the Greek army so that I can fight against the Persians who are coming back to attack us, so the rumours say. It has been ten years since we won the war against them at Marathon. Father told me not to worry about that but I saw his face cloud over when I mentioned it.

I want to be great at archery so that I can fight the Persians.

January 24

Father allowed me to attend the supper and symposium tonight that he held for the leaders of Athens. Sicinnus served us, with the help of two of the young slave boys.

Father is one of the most important men in Athens. He is a merchant but the leaders of Athens listen to him. He's very clever. These important men often come to dinner here.

Not everyone in Athens can afford to entertain like this. We must be one of the wealthiest families in Athens. We live well I think, compared to most.

One of father's friends demanded that we entertain them. Father asked Archie to sing and then I had to recite my favourite part of the Iliad. I chose the bit where Achilles

When the leaders of Athens come to dinner they sit with Father in the andron where they eat and drink wine.

quarrels with King Agamemnon and demands that he let the kidnapped Chryseis go back to her father.

They clapped but then I had to explain why I'd chosen that part. I said that it was because Achilles was doing right despite having to correct his King for his bad judgement and behaviour. There was a long debate after that, as to the merits of Agamemnon's case. I stood up for Achilles and they listened.

When I was dismissed to bed, father said that I'd argued well and he was proud of me. One day I'll be as great an orator as my father.

This coin shows an owl, an emblem of Athena, patron goddess of Athens.

April 5
(the year of the 75th Olympiad)

I never want a day like this again. I was sick all night and was too ill to go to school. Sicinnus said I should stay in bed and sleep. Father agreed then he went off hunting. Sicinnus went to school with Archie and Pol, leaving me with mother and my sisters.

By noon I was allowed to sit in the courtyard and watch the comings and goings. Italia came and sat beside me. She seemed miserable.

'Tell me about the sea,' she said, all of a sudden. I was amazed, until I remembered that she had never been outside the city-walls and hardly ever left the house and courtyard.

'Well, the sea is blue and big and wet,' I joked but she didn't laugh. Instead she began to cry and then grabbed hold of my tunic and pleaded with me to take her to the harbour at Piraeus so that she could see it for herself.

I said she was crazy – girls just weren't allowed to go out! But she wouldn't listen. She started jumping up and down with excitement.

'I'll dress as a boy. Then nobody will know!'

'Italia, forget it! Even if you were dressed as a boy your hair would give you away.'

Her answer to that was to sprint off indoors. I laid back

in the sun and prayed to Athena to endow my sister with a bit more wisdom. It didn't work.

Suddenly there was a tug at my sleeve and there stood a beautiful boy with short hair looking very like my sister.

'Italia,' I whispered in horror.
She shook herself free of my hold.

'Take me to Piraeus,' she commanded.

After that act of courage how could I refuse.

'Come Jason, the sea and your ship Argo awaits,' I answered and hauled her up.

It was easy, too easy. The gate porter waved as we left arm in arm. We went through the south gate without being stopped.

Italia and I raced each other most of the way, though she would sometimes stop quite suddenly, caught up in the beauty and wonder of all she could see. It was of small interest to me, just the olive groves, rocks, pasture and mountains in the background.

It was good to see her enjoying herself so much. She'd pay sure enough when mother saw that she'd cut off her hair.

If she was impressed by the countryside, her first sight of the sea took the breath from her. She just stood and stared and stared.

'Come on!' I shouted and dragged her on at a run down to the wide curve of the harbour.

In the Greek myth about Jason and the Golden Fleece, Jason has a ship built to take him on his voyages. He calls the ship Argo and this stone relief shows it being constructed.

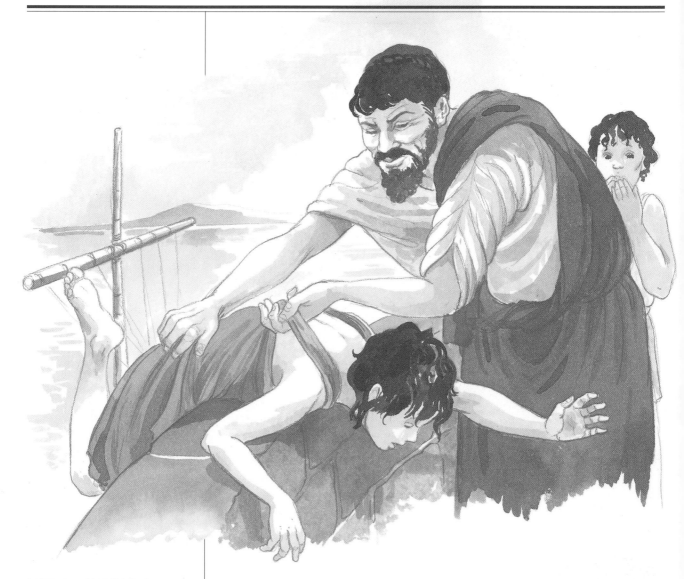

We sat on the harbour wall, the rocking triremes anchored below us. We watched the water heave and fall in the light breeze.

'I wish I could sail away for ever,' she breathed.
'Like Odysseus returning to Penelope, only you're Odysseus and I'm Penelope weaving at my loom!' I joked.

She smiled.

'Cleo!' came a loud deep shout from the warehouses opposite us. Italia looked at me and we both panicked. It was father and he was striding towards us!

Italia jumped off the wall to the ground but at the same time shoved me over the other side! I can swim but there was a mast length drop to the decks of the ships. I'd have been killed for certain if I hadn't managed to cling by the finger tips to the edge of the wall.

'Get me up!' I screamed but Italia hissed 'Shh!'

Everything turned out well for Penelope, who kept her suitors at bay by unpicking her weaving until Odysseus returned, but I wasn't sure things would turn out so well for Italia and me.

This vase shows our famous ships called triremes.

Father's face appeared over the wall. He was grinning and all he could say was, 'Is this clinging to walls a new Games event I haven't yet heard about?'

Very funny!

'Help!' I gasped, as my fingers slipped from their perilous hold.

Father reached down, grabbed me by the arm and belt and yanked me up and over the wall, leaving me beached like a whale on the ground at his feet.

'Suppose you tell me why you and your friend are here when you are too sick to go to school' Father suggested.

There was amusement in his voice but I was shocked by my close escape and angry with Italia. I could see her sandled feet not more than a javelin's length from me and she was starting to run away! That did it. I jumped up and lunged after her to try to stop her. We fell to the ground. The next thing I knew Father was pulling me off and hoisting Italia up. She was lighter than he expected and they came face to face.

Father stepped away, puzzled, then grabbed Italia's chin and stared at her.

He let her go with a push and turned to glare at me. There was no more fun in his eyes and I was scared. He yelled for his horse and one of the slaves came running with it.

'I'm taking Italia home, Cleo. You can walk. It will give you the time you need to find some explanation for this!'

He wrapped her about with his cloak, mounted his horse and in one rough move dragged her up to sit in front of him.

That walk turned out to be the longest and most miserable I have ever had to make. I felt sick again and my mind went blank. All I could see was father's blazing eyes.

When I dragged myself through the doorway the porter told me to go straight to father in the living room. He was there with Sicinnus who was holding a stick. For once I wished I was small again so that mother could protect me.

I came to a wary halt out of reach. No one said anything at first. Finally I raised my eyes to father and feebly tried to explain.

He listened, unmoved. Then he coldly said 'Give me three logical reasons why I shouldn't have Sicinnus beat you, Cleo.'

Rapidly I tried to come up with three logical reasons for me getting away with this.

Father waited. Sicinnus was distracting me by thumping the stick into the palm of his hand. 'First,' I began with a rather shaky voice. 'First I do not need to be punished for taking Italia to Piraeus. I know I should not have done it so hitting me with a stick is not necessary to make me see my fault.'

'Second, I protected her from any harm and any disgrace. Therefore I acted with honour and with due regard for her reputation.'

Father tensed a little and his eyebrows narrowed. I was losing the argument, I could tell. I desperately tried to come up with a better reason.

'Finally... finally, if Achilles can hide amongst the daughters of King Lykomedes, disguised as a girl, why cannot Italia disguise herself as a boy and walk for once amongst men without fault?'

I stopped. Father looked at me for a very long time. When he spoke it was almost as bad as the cutting edge of a whip.

'Your logic is faulty boy! First your punishment is to deter not inform. Second there was no honour in your behaviour today. Third, while a man may lower himself to the level of a woman, a woman can never rise to the heights of man. It is beyond her.'

I'd lost.

The walk back from Piraeus to Athens seemed to go on forever. Father had been so cross and I was frightened of facing him.

Sicinnus looked at me. He wasn't angry but that would not save me any blows. I looked away.

Moving towards me, he forced me onto my hands and knees. He raised the stick, then father whispered, 'No, Sicinnus. Leave him. His logic was poor but for his age it was well reasoned. Your mind and tongue have saved your skin Cleo. Remember that!'

I staggered to my feet and must have stood like some dumb beast for it took Sicinnus' rough push to send me on my way. I ran to my room and hid.

I went to supper. I had to, I was starving. Everyone was quiet. Father was out to supper much to my relief but mother was fierce-eyed.

After supper, Archie dragged me to our bedroom and told me that mother had beaten Italia. She wasn't even given the chance to explain. Archie was furious with me. I tried to tell him what had happened but he wouldn't listen. I gave up and went to bed.

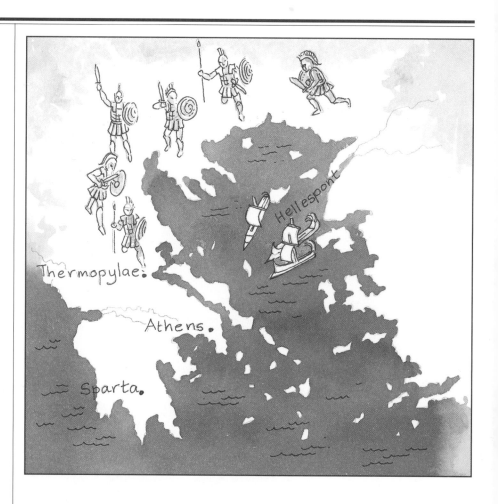

June 22

Athens is rife with talk of the Persians. King Xerxes is crossing from Hellespont with a large army and fleet. Father is trying to rally the citizens and organize some kind of defence. There was an assembly meeting called in the Agora this morning. Father said it broke up in chaos. People are afraid.

June 25

One of my friends, Nic, told me today that Sicinnus shouldn't be trusted because he's a Persian. He told me that all my family could be killed in our beds by him. I should watch him carefully.

I told him he was wrong, Sicinnus would never betray us. He laughed at me so I punched him but Sicinnus had seen us and came over to stop us fighting. I couldn't look him in the eye. What if Nic was right?

Father came to me when I was in bed and very quietly asked me what I had fought about. I didn't want to tell him but I had to in the end. He was angry with me.

'Am I a fool?' he said sharply.

When I shook my head he held my chin and said, 'No, Cleo, I am not a fool. I trust Sicinnus and so will you.'

He left after that. He must be right, he must!

July 8

The Panathenaea festival has begun. I was looking forward to it because I'm competing in the boys equestrian sprint but it isn't the same as last year. People are worried and all the talk is of the successes of the Persians to the north. Father is rarely at home now. He is in charge of the Athenian navy, though the Spartans are demanding the leadership. I don't understand this and Sicinnus won't explain. He won't even talk of it.

If the Persians come to Athens and capture us Sicinnus would be freed. I don't want him to go.

The Panathenaea festival is held in honour of Athena.

July 12

I didn't win my race today. I am cross with myself. I should have done better.

Archie is going with his coach to train with the officials at Olympia. All the athletes have to go for a month before the Games start, to make sure no one is cheating. Father was going to take Pol and me to watch the Games but now we can't go. The Persians are marching south.

July 27

The site of the games at Olympia.

Father made a very important speech at the assembly meeting today. He's persuaded the citizens to agree to send away the women and children to Troizen. Xerxes is heading for Athens.

When father got home he called the family together to tell us that we'd be leaving. Mother refused to go.

'When I see flames rising from the houses in the town, then I'll leave my house, but not until then!' she stated and nothing father could do or say shifted her. I've never seen father so angry or mother so determined.

August 22

A statue of Leonidas still stands at the Pass of Thermopylae.

August 30

Word came today that the Persians were trapped at the Pass of Thermopylae. The Spartan leader Leonidas held them there for two days, before all the Spartan soldiers died along with the brave Leonidas. The Persians are through the Pass and are unstoppable.

Sicinnus is away with father. Mother has sent most of the slaves to Grandfather's farm on the island of Salamis. Mother says we'll go there too if we have to leave. She's got everything organized but I can't help wishing we'd done as father said and left earlier.

Pol and I have been practising with toy swords and knives. I'm not very good at fighting but I've got to try. I know where father keeps the weapons and Pol and I will fight to protect our family.

Father sailed in to Piraeus today with the Greek fleet just in time to stop a full-scale panic. Pol and I had gone to the Agora to buy some provisions for mother and while we were there, word went up that the Persians were in sight. People ran in all directions creating chaos.

Suddenly I heard father's voice rise above the frenzied cries ordering silence. The crowd was restless and scared but stood still and listened. 'Citizens of Athens, listen. The Persians are still far away but we have heard from a runner that they are expected to reach Athens in the next two days. We must act now to protect our families and property. The only way we can do that is by thinking not screaming!'

'I have the entire allied fleet at Piraeus, more than enough to transport all of you to the island of Salamis. The priests will stay to defend the Acropolis and those citizens left should be ready to man the boats and fight when we need. We can win, citizens but only if we keep calm. Trust me!'

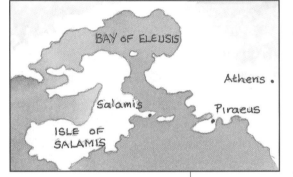

Father told them they were to go home and wait for instructions from the officials of the city to leave. They were then to make their way down to the harbour.

Sicinnus was suddenly at our side. I hugged him but he was brisk.

'Come home now. I've to see you boarded on your father's ship before nightfall.'

We went as fast as we could. Mother gave us a long hug when we got home. While Sicinnus saw to the loading up of the cart we sat with Italia and Syb in the courtyard. We were all frightened but there was nothing we could do but wait. It seemed like forever before the cart returned for us at dusk. The driver said that there was chaos down at the harbour. Father had sent his ship out into the bay and we were to be taken out in a row boat from the beach.

We clambered onto the cart, grateful to be leaving at last. There were all sorts of people hurrying down on foot. All around us were lost and freed pets, dogs, cats, rabbits, hens, colts, donkeys and snorting horses. I have never seen the streets so busy.

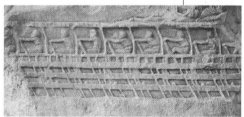

The Greek ships were gathering just outside the harbour, the sea seemed covered with triremes.

When we got to the beach, we scrambled through the shallows and climbed on the waiting rowing boat. Sicinnus took his place beside the boatman. They would both row to make better speed.

It was already dark but in the distance we could see flaming arrows begin to sear across the skyline into the city. The Persian attack had begun.

I clutched my heart and tried to stop shaking. The boat lurched into motion and we began to pull away from the shallows, heading towards father's ship.

The Persian archers sent burning arrows towards Athens ... the battle had begun!

September 4

For days now Athens has been under attack. The wooden palisades around the Acropolis are ablaze. The city is in flames. There can be nothing left of our home just ashes and blackened stone.

The girls have gone with mother to the farm but Pol and I are staying at the camp with father. We keep out of the way but he lets us sleep in his tent. There are endless talks between the commanders of the fleets and armies – nothing but wrangling and shouting. I wish they would just do something to stop the Persians.

September 15

The Acropolis has fallen. We are surely lost and the gods have forgotten us. What have we done wrong to bring this disaster on us?

It is hard to stop feeling miserable. Pol keeps busy by memorising some of the Odyssey. I shall learn it with him if I can.

September 18

Father is trying to convince the Spartan commander-in-chief and the other officers that a plan he has to defeat the Persians will work.

Father is always right about these things, they've got to follow his advice, they've just got to, otherwise we'll be trapped here and the Persians will come and kill us all.

Spartan warriors are very formidable. They could be important allies if they agree with Father's plans.

September 19

What a night! I don't know what made me wake but it was pitch dark when I did and someone was moving outside the tent. Pol was fast asleep, and both father and Sicinnus were missing.

I got up and taking my knife, crept out into the night. The cloudy sky did not let much moonlight through and so I stumbled over the rocks in the pitch dark heading towards the distant sound of lowered voices. I could just make out two figures heading for the beach.

Then in a fleeting moment of moonlight I recognised one of them. The shadowy figure ahead of me, stooping over an anchored boat, was Sicinnus.

I couldn't believe it. He was escaping, back to his Persian masters over the water! My friend Nic was right after all. A terrible shudder ran through me. 'He's a spy,' I thought. 'No, it can't be! Not Sicinnus! It can't!'

The small boat was pushed away from the shingle. The other man withdrew into the shadows. I ran, ran for the boat, ran to stop Sicinnus!

I splashed through the waves and lunged full length at the huddled man in the boat. He shrugged me off as if I'd been a dirty cloak. I fell heavily into the boat. It rocked violently as I scrambled to get up.

Suddenly there was a blade at my throat and I froze.

My life flashed before me as I felt a dagger at my throat.

'Go back!' Sicinnus hissed, sheathing his knife.

'Sicinnus!' I cried.

He clapped his hand ferociously over my mouth, scooped me up as if I was as light as a feather and threw me overboard, into the shallows.

By the time I'd got my legs under me, the boat had gone, only the occasional splash of the oars marked its passage.

I held my head in my hands and then dragged myself out dripping wet and in despair.

'Cleo,' came a familiar voice from the darkness. I ran toward the sound. It was my father. I tried to find the words to tell father that Sicinnus had gone but he silenced me.

'Cleo, Sicinnus is going to the Persian forces under my orders. It's a trick, boy, a dangerous, deadly and vital trick but a trick nonetheless. Sicinnus won't betray us.'

I wished I could be sure. Father went back to the tent with me and settled me down to sleep. He didn't go to his own bed but sat reading by the light of an oil lamp. The last thing I saw was him turn his page.

If Father's plan to outwit King Xerxes works, we may be safe from the Persians yet.

Father woke me early and took me out on to the hillside to talk. He tried to explain that Sicinnus had to convince the Persian King Xerxes that the Greek fleet was about to flee. Father was hoping that Xerxes would move his ships into the straits to stop us. Then we would attack. It seemed to be madness but father just smiled and said, 'Don't tell me my own son doubts my thinking in this?' I held him tight, unable to answer. He stroked my head and answered.

'Athena is with us, Cleo. If you can't trust me, trust her. She protects her own.'
I sighed and nodded.

'Don't say anything about this to anyone, not even Pol', he ordered.

A messenger was approaching. Father said no more. I drifted away, knowing he wanted that, and then he left me on the hillside. He had work to do.

September 20

Father is so important that coins have been made showing his picture.

I awoke before dawn unable to sleep any longer and shook Pol awake. Nobody else was around so we knew something was afoot. We ran to the crest of the hill. The sight we saw took our breath away. The sea was covered with ships. We could see a line of our ships with Father's flag-ship right in the middle but there were hundreds of Persian ships coming towards them. We were hopelessly outnumbered. Some of our ships were drawing backwards between the mainland and the island. What was Father doing? Surely he wasn't going to flee from the Persians now?

We seemed to be watching for ages – I've never seen so many ships, there must have been about 1,000 Persian vessels advancing. I was beginning to despair when suddenly our battle-hymn blasted out. Some of our ships had got to the sides of the Persian fleet and were forcing them into the middle of the channel, cramming them in so that they couldn't move! Pol and I watched as the ships rammed each other, crashing

and breaking up under the soldiers and sailors feet. The noise of wood splintering was deafening as our ships rammed into the unarmoured sides of the Persian ships. There was fighting, hand to hand on the lurching decks. It looked horrendous and was terrifying.

We ran down to the sea, hoping to help our Greek sailors as they tried to swim to the shore. We arrived at the water's edge to find hacked and bleeding bodies all about. The lapping water was foaming and stained with blood.

Our soldiers were standing in the shallows picking off the struggling Persians and killing them. I know they are our enemies but kept thinking of Sicinnus. Surely father wouldn't want this?

Suddenly the sound of screams and grinding, splintering wood ripped through the air. A pair of interlocked ships lurched toward the rocks in the shallows, completely out of control.

Before our eyes were thousands of ships crashing into each other in the narrow strait between the island and the mainland.

Men, instead of fighting, threw themselves overboard and tried to save their lives by reaching the shore. One of the Persians splashed close to Pol. To my horror Pol took out his knife and lunged at the man already half dead from drowning.

I screamed and threw myself across the sailor's body. Pol only just missed me, then tried to kick me off.

'No, no. Leave him!' I shouted.

Pol stared at me in disbelief. I didn't wait, but started to drag the nearly unconscious man to the shore. He was extremely heavy but eventually I managed to get him behind the rocks, so that the soldiers wouldn't see him.

Pol had already gone off to join the soldiers in their killing. I tossed the man's weapons into the sea.

'What have you got there?!' a man shouted harshly at me. He was standing over me, on one of the rocks, blood dripping from his sword.

'He's mine! A prisoner of war and my slave now!' I yelled with as much authority as I could muster.

The man laughed. 'Well tie him up then, boy!'

He tossed a thin cord beside me then hearing a call for help, he ran off.

As I tied the Persian's wrists he stirred. He struggled for a moment then collapsed. Pol appeared.

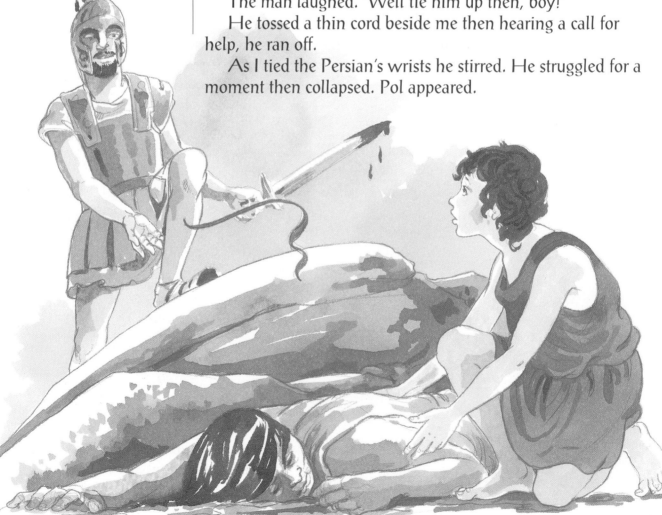

'Got yourself a prize then, little brother! Come on, I'll give you a hand getting him back to the tent.'

We dragged the man up and got him back home. He was tied up outside and left to rest.

Suddenly there was the rousing sound of laughter and cheering. Father strode in, alive and filthy dirty. He snatched us off our feet and swung us about.

'We've won! We've done it!'

The men took him off to celebrate, leaving us breathless but very happy.

September 21

The Persians are pulling back. Father says they'll march home now that autumn is coming. I had to give my prisoner over to father. He sold him and gave me the money. I hope he'll be alright.

September 24

We're being sent to the farm today. Father won't let us go with him to Athens tomorrow. I told him we could look after ourselves but he wouldn't listen. He doesn't understand but I must look for Sicinnus. I told Pol I'd run away and get to Athens on my own. He told me I was being stupid.

September 25

One day I'll fire arrows as well as any Greek soldier with Sicinnus to teach me.

Pol and I were just climbing into the cart to go to the farm, when an arrow landed in the dirt nearby. I looked up and saw Sicinnus. I ran to him and gave him a long hug.

'I thought you'd gone forever' I said.

'How could I leave you?' he answered with a grin, 'You're far too poor at archery yet. When you fire arrows as well as me I'll release you from my care, in the mean time move over, I've orders to see you safely to the farm.'

Everything will be alright now. I know it!

Glossary

Acropolis	This can just mean a high place but in Athens the Acropolis was a very high plateau above the city, on which stood the temples to the gods and in particular the temple of Athena, the city's founding goddess. It was very important.
Agora	A market place and central square where assemblies were often held. The main officials worked here.
amphora	A large clay pot to hold wine or other liquids such as olive oil.
andron	A room where the men meet to eat and discuss.
archery	The skill of firing arrows from a bow to kill, used in war and hunting.
archon	An elected leader, like a mayor, chosen or selected by lot to run the city for the citizens.
Athena	Goddess of Wisdom and Athens.
beacons	Burning fires on hilltops lit to pass on a warning of invasion.
equestrian	To do with horses, for example an equestrian sprint would involve riding a horse in a race.
gym	A public group of buildings where sports are practised.
Iliad	An important long poem, written by an Ancient Greek writer called Homer about Greek heroes such as Achilles at the siege of Troy. All Greek children and men would know the stories.
Jason	A legendary hero in Greek mythology.
javelin	A long thin spear, used in battle and in sport.
Odyssey	A poem by Homer which describes the adventures of Odysseus on his return to Ithaca after the siege of Troy.
olive grove	A small orchard where olive trees are planted.
Olympic Games	A sports event with religious ceremonies held every four years at Olympia in southern Greece.
palaestra	A wrestling school or gymnasium
palisades	Fencing around a mound of earth used to keep people out, like a sturdy fence.
Panathenaea	An annual festival in honour of Athena, goddess of Athens.
pasture	Grassy slopes where animals graze.
Spartan	A member of the city-state of Sparta. Spartans had a reputation for being extremely good fighters. Sometimes they fought against the Athenians; sometimes they fought with them, for example when the Persians were attacking.
stadium	An area where sports events were held.
symposium	A dinner party exclusively for men where the main entertainment was discussion and argument between the guests.
triremes	Small wooden ships used for carrying cargo and for fighting at sea. Powered by sail and rowers.
warehouse	A building in which goods are stored.